BARACK OBAMA

By Geoffrey M. Horn

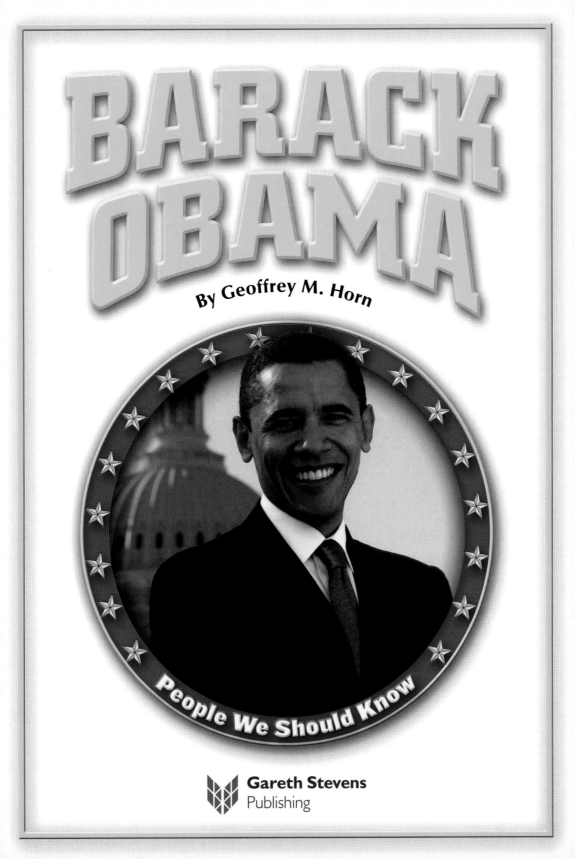

People We Should Know

Gareth Stevens
Publishing

Please visit our web site at **www.garethstevens.com**.
For a free color catalog describing our list of high-quality books,
call 1-800-542-2595 (USA) or 1-800-387-3178 (Canada). Our fax: 1-877-542-2596

Library of Congress Cataloging-in-Publication Data
Horn, Geoffrey M.
    Barack Obama / by Geoffrey M. Horn.
      p. cm. — (People we should know)
    Includes bibliographical references and index.
    ISBN-10: 1-4339-0017-3   ISBN-13: 978-1-4339-0017-4 (lib. bdg.)
    ISBN-10: 1-4339-0157-9   ISBN-13: 978-1-4339-0157-7 (softcover)
    1. Obama, Barack—Juvenile literature.   2. African American legislators—Biography—
Juvenile literature.   3. Legislators—United States—Biography—Juvenile literature.
    4. United States. Congress. Senate—Biography—Juvenile literature.   5. Presidential
candidates—United States—Biography—Juvenile literature.   6. Racially mixed people—
United States—Biography—Juvenile literature. I. Title.
    E901.1.O23H67   2009
    328.73092—dc22[B]   2008043313

This edition first published in 2009 by
Gareth Stevens Publishing
A Weekly Reader® Company
1 Reader's Digest Road
Pleasantville, NY 10570-7000 USA

Executive Managing Editor: Lisa M. Herrington
Senior Editor: Brian Fitzgerald
Associate Editor: Amanda Hudson
Creative Director: Lisa Donovan
Senior Designer: Keith Plechaty
Production Designer: Cynthia Malaran
Photo Researcher: Kim Babbitt
Publisher: Keith Garton

Picture credits
Cover and title page: Courtesy of Senator Obama's office; p. 5: Rick Wilking/Reuters/Corbis;
pp. 7, 10, 15, 18, 19, 20, 25: AP Images; pp. 9, 13: Polaris Images; pp. 11, 17: Newscom;
p. 23: Scott Olsen/Getty Images; p. 26: Jemal Countess/Getty Images; p. 27: AFP/Getty Images;
p. 28: John Zich/Corbis.

Printed in the United States of America

3 4 5 6 7 8 9 10 09

TABLE OF CONTENTS

Words in the glossary appear in **bold** type
the first time they are used in the text.

CHAPTER 1

"We Are One People"

On the night of July 27, 2004, Barack Obama delivered the speech that changed his life. He was only 42 years old and a state senator from Illinois. Few people outside his home state knew his name or what he looked like.

All that was about to change. Soon, his words would be heard by thousands of people at the 2004 Democratic **National Convention** in Boston, Massachusetts. Millions more would watch the speech on TV.

Barack Obama speaks at the Democratic National Convention in Boston, Massachusetts, in 2004.

A Powerful Moment

As Obama waited to speak to the crowd, many thoughts passed through his mind. He thought of his father, a black man from Africa. He thought of his mother, a white woman from Kansas. Neither would see his big speech. His father had died in a car crash in 1982. His mother had lost a battle with cancer in 1995. The name *Barack* means "blessed." Obama wished his parents could have lived to see just how blessed his life had become.

Fast Fact

Obama has a sense of humor about himself. He has described himself as "a tall, skinny guy with big ears and a funny name."

> **❝** There's not a black America and white America and Latino America and Asian America. There's the United States of America. **❞**
>
> —Barack Obama at the 2004 National Convention

Setting the Tone

Obama had been chosen to give the convention's **keynote speech**. A keynote speech is about the political party's ideas and values. During his speech, Obama told the crowd that "we are connected as one people."

Obama said his own background showed that people from different countries and cultures can come together. Americans hold different political ideas and religious views. In an election, some politicians focus on the things that divide us. Obama said that was wrong. As Americans, he said, we need to focus on the values we share.

A Lot Can Change in Eight Years!

Barack Obama came a long way in a short time. He attended his first Democratic National Convention in Los Angeles, California, in 2000. He knew few people and felt like a stranger.

His second convention was in Boston in 2004. Then, he was a state senator. He was running for the U.S. **Senate**. After he gave the keynote speech, he was one of the party's brightest stars. His third convention was in Denver, Colorado, in 2008 (above). He left the convention as his party's choice for president of the United States.

Historic Moment

When Obama finished speaking, the crowd cheered. Millions of Americans were moved by what he said. Almost overnight, Obama changed from a little-known Illinois politician to one of the most admired people in the United States. Four years later, in November 2008, he was elected president of the United States. He is the first African American to hold that office.

CHAPTER 2

Beginnings

Barack Obama was born in Hawaii, the nation's youngest state. People of many different races live there. In 1960, nearly half of the states in the United States banned racially mixed marriages. But Hawaii was a place where people of different backgrounds felt free to mingle and marry.

In 1959, the same year Hawaii became a state, Barack's parents met at the University of Hawaii in Honolulu. His mother's full name was Stanley Ann Dunham, but most people called her Ann. Ann was born in Kansas in 1942, and she lived in many places as a child. "She was a very intelligent, quiet girl," one of her friends said later.

Ann Dunham holds her young son, Barack, in Hawaii.

A New Family

Barack's father, Barack Hussein Obama, came from Kenya, a country in East Africa. He was the first African student to attend the University of Hawaii. A member of the Luo tribe, he had herded goats as a child. Barack Sr.'s father was a chief in their home village.

Ann and Barack were married on February 2, 1961. On August 4, Ann gave birth to a son. Barack and Ann named their child Barack Hussein Obama II.

Fast Fact

Stanley Ann Dunham got her name from her father. He had been hoping for a son!

Moving On

In 1963, Barack Sr. went to study at Harvard University in Massachusetts. He left Ann and Barack behind in Hawaii. Ann divorced him early in 1964. Later, he returned home to Kenya. Ann and little Barack were on their own.

Obama saw his father only once after 1963—when the Kenyan visited Hawaii in 1971. Much later, Obama would talk about how important it was for him to be a better father to his own children.

Fast Fact

In 1995, Obama called his first book *Dreams from My Father*.

Little Barack shows his tricycle-riding talents in Hawaii.

Gramps and Toot

Ann's parents were Stanley and Madelyn Dunham. They were married in Kansas in 1940. Stanley fought in **World War II**. Madelyn worked in a factory that made B-29 bombers for the U.S. war effort.

Ann's parents lived in Hawaii while their grandson was growing up. Barack called his grandfather "Gramps" and his grandmother "Toot." The nickname comes from *tutu*, which means "grandmother" in the Hawaiian language. Gramps and Toot helped care for Barack after his father went back to Kenya.

Stanley Dunham and Barack

Bending the Rules

Life was hard for Obama's mother in the early 1960s. Ann was a single mom with little money. She bought groceries with **food stamps**. "She was the kindest, most generous spirit I have ever known," Obama wrote years later. "What is best in me I owe to her."

Ann worked hard to get her college degree from the University of Hawaii. While she studied, her parents took care of their grandson. The family called him "Barry" or "Bar" when he was young.

CHAPTER 3

Finding Himself

At the University of Hawaii, Ann had met a fellow student named Lolo Soetoro. Lolo came from Indonesia, a large island nation in the Pacific. Ann and Lolo were married in 1967 and moved to Indonesia. Barry lived and went to school there for the next four years. His classmates knew him as Barry Soetoro.

Ann and Lolo had a daughter, Maya, in 1970. Maya looked up to Barry. "He was a *great* big brother," she says.

Nine-year-old Barack poses with his mother, stepfather, and baby sister, Maya.

Growing Pains

Barry had a hard time fitting in with his classmates. He struggled with the language. He was bigger than other boys, who teased him about his size. They also teased him about his skin color, which was darker than theirs.

Like most Indonesians, Lolo was **Muslim**. On major Muslim holidays, Barry went with Lolo to a **mosque**. But he also took classes at a Catholic school. There he learned how to be a Christian.

Fast Fact

In Indonesia, Barry had an ape named Tata as a pet!

A Lesson From Lolo

After Barry lost a fight with an Indonesian boy, Lolo bought him boxing gloves. Lolo wanted to teach his stepson how to defend himself.

Lolo asked Barry whether he wanted to be weak or strong. Then he answered his own question. "Better to be strong," he said. "If you can't be strong, be clever and make peace with someone who's strong. But always better to be strong yourself. Always."

More Changes

After a few years, Ann and Lolo started having problems in their marriage. Ann and Barry went back to Hawaii in 1971. He started going to the Punahou School. Few African American kids went there.

When Barry was a teenager, Ann decided to return to Indonesia to do research. Barry stayed in Honolulu. He lived with Gramps and Toot.

During that period, painful questions began to bother him. Was he Barry or Barack? Soetoro or Obama? Black or white? Christian or Muslim? He became confused. His grades fell, and he started getting into trouble. He needed to get his life together.

Fast Fact

Obama loved to bodysurf in Hawaii. Bodysurfers ride the waves without using a surfboard.

From Barry to Barack

The change didn't happen overnight. But slowly Obama began to learn more about himself and his background. He studied harder. He read books by famous African American writers. He started calling himself Barack—his father's strong African name.

At the same time, he held fast to the values he had learned from his mother. "Fortunately, I think that my family had such strong values," he said. "I pulled out of that funk and was able to succeed."

"O'Bomber"

Obama played basketball at the Punahou School. His teammates nicknamed him "O'Bomber" because of his double-pump jump shot. Obama's coach says that he was a hardworking player. "I can remember him being here early and playing before school," he says. "I remember him bouncing his ball, books in one hand, ball in the other hand."

Obama still loves playing basketball. His favorite team is the Chicago Bulls.

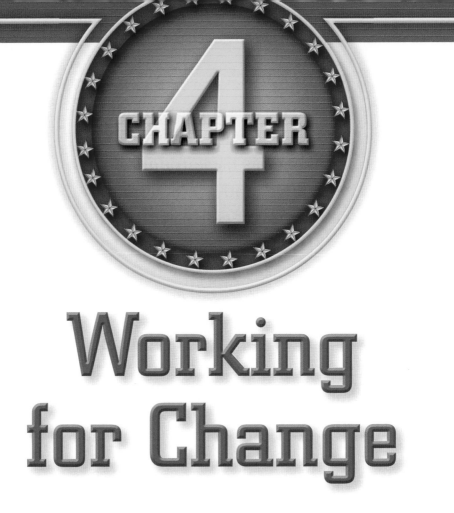

CHAPTER 4

Working for Change

In 1979, Obama moved to Los Angeles, California. There he took classes at Occidental College. The school had a program that allowed some students to switch to Columbia University in New York City. After two years at Occidental, Obama was accepted to Columbia. He studied politics, earning his college degree in 1983.

In college, Obama had a lot of ideas about how people could change the world. Now it was time to test those ideas.

In the early 1980s, Barack takes a break from Columbia to enjoy some New York City sights.

On the South Side

In the mid-1980s, Obama took a job as a **community organizer**. He worked with low-income families on the South Side of Chicago, Illinois. The area had been hit hard when steel factories closed. People needed job training. They also wanted better schools, safer streets, and better playgrounds for their children. Obama got families, church groups, businesses, and local officials to work together. He showed people how they could work to make their lives better.

Meeting Michelle

In 1988, Obama began studying law at Harvard University. When he took a summer job with a Chicago law firm in 1989, he met his summer adviser—a tall young woman named Michelle Robinson.

Barack did not make a great first impression on Michelle. He was late for their first meeting. But she changed her mind about him after he urged her to come to one of his community meetings. "This guy is different," she thought to herself. "He's got a seriousness and commitment you don't see every day."

Michelle waves to the crowd at the 2008 Democratic National Convention.

Michelle Obama

Michelle Obama received her college degree from Princeton University in 1985. She earned a law degree from Harvard in 1988. Like her husband, she worked as a community organizer in Chicago. She also worked for the Chicago Mayor's Office and held a high-ranking job with the University of Chicago Hospitals. She took a break from her job to help her husband run for president in 2008.

Learning the Law

Obama studied at Harvard, the same school his father had attended, until 1991. One of his teachers was Laurence Tribe, a famous expert on the law. In 2007, Tribe called Barack the "best student I ever had." Obama was president of the *Harvard Law Review*. He was the first African American to earn that honor.

Michelle and Barack are all smiles on their wedding day in 1992.

After receiving his law degree, Obama returned to live in Chicago. He and Michelle were married in October 1992. Their wedding took place at Trinity United Church of Christ. Obama had joined the church on Chicago's South Side in the late 1980s. The Obamas have two daughters. Malia was born in 1998. Sasha was born in 2001.

Obama teaches a class at the University of Chicago in the early 1990s.

Getting Out the Vote

The 1990s brought many other changes in Obama's life. He started teaching law in 1992 at the University of Chicago. He also began to rise in Chicago politics. In 1992, he ran a program that signed up nearly 150,000 new voters. Four years later, he ran for a seat in the Illinois state **legislature**. He was only 35, but he had already been working in the community for many years. He had made many friends and won many admirers during that period. They helped him win a state senate seat in 1996.

A Bump in the Road

One of Obama's goals in running for office was to clean up state government. He passed a **bill** in the senate to make sure senators were more honest. He also worked to improve health care for people in Illinois.

In 2000, Obama ran for a seat in the U.S. **House of Representatives**. The man he ran against—Bobby Rush—had held the seat since 1993. Rush had a lot of support on the South Side. Michelle didn't want Barack to run against him. Some of Barack's friends also thought it was a bad idea. They were right. He lost. But he had never backed down from a challenge before. After the election, he went back to work in the state senate. He kept his sights on higher office.

> **"**I'm from Chicago. I know politics. I'm skinny but I'm tough.**"**
>
> –Barack Obama

CHAPTER 5

"Yes We Can!"

In the fall of 2002, the United States was getting ready to go to war with Iraq. Not many people spoke out against the war then. Obama was one of the few elected officials to oppose it. He gave a passionate speech explaining his beliefs to nearly 2,000 people at Chicago's Federal Plaza.

After the war began, Obama praised the American troops who fought in Iraq. Still, he continued to believe that the war was a mistake. The war was one of the issues that he promised to take on when he ran for the U.S. Senate in 2004. He traveled around the state, talking to voters about the issues that mattered to them.

With Malia watching, Obama casts his vote in the November 2004 election.

Running for the U.S. Senate

Obama had already won a **party primary** in the Senate race when he gave his keynote speech in July 2004. He had shown that he knew how to connect with voters of different races and backgrounds.

Obama was elected to the Senate in November 2004 with 70 percent of the vote. He was the only African American in the Senate.

Down to Business

After his Senate win, Obama got a lot of attention from the media. One of his first tasks when he came to Washington, D.C., in January 2005 was to try to make government more honest. He also worked to prevent nuclear weapons from falling into the hands of people who wanted to harm the United States.

Eyes on the White House

Obama had been in the Senate for only two years when he decided to run for president. At the time, the war in Iraq was not going well. The economy was sagging. Polls showed that many Americans wanted change. Obama said he could bring people together to make it happen. Change became the major theme of his **campaign**.

66 Together, we will change this country and change the world. **99**

—Barack Obama, during his campaign for president

Family Rules

Raising a family can be hard when parents are on the road as much as Barack and Michelle. They try to keep the rules simple. The girls have to set their own alarm clocks at night, get themselves up in the morning, and make their own beds every day.

Malia plays soccer and dances. Sasha does gymnastics. Both girls take piano and tennis lessons. When things get hectic, Michelle's mother has always been willing to help out.

Barack walks on the beach with Malia (left) and Sasha (right).

Spreading the Word

Obama built his campaign slowly, beginning in early 2007. By late fall, he was starting to attract huge crowds. Many college students and other young people came to his **rallies**. His speeches also attracted older people who had never cared much about politics. His campaign raised more than a half billion dollars. No other **candidate** for public office in the United States has ever raised that much money.

Help From His Friends

Many famous people helped Obama in his campaign. Talk show host Oprah Winfrey (left) was an important early supporter. She campaigned with him in December 2007 at large rallies in Iowa, New Hampshire, and South Carolina.

Jay-Z put on free concerts in support of Obama. Many other celebrities, including LeBron James, Jennifer Aniston, Chris Rock, and Matt Damon, contributed to his campaign.

Making History

To become his party's choice for president, Obama had to defeat several well-known Democrats. His toughest opponent in the party primaries was Senator Hillary Clinton from New York. She is a former **first lady**.

The 2008 party primaries were an exciting time. If Clinton won, a woman would have a chance to become president. If Obama won, an African American would have the same chance. Obama won. Support from young voters played a big part in his victory.

John McCain and Obama share their ideas about the country's future during a debate in September 2008.

Tough Race

Obama was the first African American ever chosen by a major party to run for president. Obama picked Senator Joe Biden from Delaware to run with him for vice president. Biden had been in the U.S. Senate for 26 years.

Republicans chose Senator John McCain from Arizona to run for president. For vice president, McCain picked Governor Sarah Palin of Alaska. Obama had three **debates** against McCain. The two men argued about what kind of change America needed.

Fast Fact

Will.i.am, Common, Scarlett Johansson, and other stars made a music video to support Obama. The song, "Yes We Can," got more than 10 million views on YouTube.

On Election Night, the Obama family celebrates Barack's historic victory.

Obama Wins!

More than 125 million people had cast their votes by the end of Election Day, November 4. Some voters stood in line for hours. When the votes were counted, Obama had defeated McCain by a wide margin. His supporters were thrilled. Many cried tears of joy that night.

"It's been a long time coming," Obama said in his acceptance speech. "But tonight, because of what we did on this date, in this election, at this defining moment, change has come to America."

Time Line

1961 — Barack Hussein Obama II is born August 4 in Honolulu, Hawaii.

1963 — Obama's father leaves his mother. Four years later, his mother marries Lolo Soetoro.

1971 — Obama returns to Hawaii. For a few years, he lives with his mother's parents.

1983 — Obama earns a degree from Columbia University.

1985 — Obama settles in Chicago, Illinois, where he works for three years as a community organizer.

1991 — Obama earns a law degree from Harvard University.

1992 — Obama marries Michelle Robinson. They later have two daughters, Malia and Sasha.

1996 — Obama wins a seat in the Illinois state legislature.

2004 — Obama delivers the keynote speech at the Democratic National Convention and wins a seat in the Senate.

2008 — Obama is elected president of the United States.

Glossary

bill: a written plan for a new law to be considered by Congress

campaign: a race between candidates for an office or position

candidate: a person who is running for office

community organizer: someone who works with a community of people, such as low-income citizens, to achieve a common goal

debates: contests in which two sides argue opposing points of view

first lady: the president's wife

food stamps: a U.S. government program that helps low-income people buy food

House of Representatives: a house of the U.S. Congress, with 435 voting members elected to two-year terms

keynote speech: a speech that sets the tone for an event

legislature: the lawmaking body of a state or country

mosque: a place where Muslims gather to pray

Muslim: a follower of Islam

national convention: a large gathering at which a political party officially announces its candidate for president

party primary: a state election in which members of a political party vote for their candidate for president

rallies: large meetings held to arouse enthusiasm

Senate: a house of the U.S. Congress, with 100 voting members elected to six-year terms

World War II: a world conflict fought from 1939 to 1945; the United States became involved in December 1941, when Japan attacked the U.S. Naval Base at Pearl Harbor, Hawaii

Find Out More

Books

Goodman, Susan. *See How They Run: Campaign Dreams, Election Schemes, and the Race to the White House.* New York: Bloomsbury, 2008.

Steele, Philip. *Vote.* New York: DK Children, 2008.

Thomas, William David. *How Do We Elect Our Leaders?* My American Government. Pleasantville, N.Y.: Gareth Stevens, 2008.

.

Web Sites

Ben's Guide to U.S. Government for Kids
www.bensguide.gpo.gov

Congress for Kids
www.congressforkids.net/index.htm

White House Kids Home Page
www.whitehouse.gov/kids

Source Notes

p. 5: "Remarks of Senator Barack Obama at the Herblock Foundation Annual Lecture." BarackObama.com. April 6, 2005. www.barackobama.com/2005/04/06/remarks_of_senator_barack_obam_1.php

p. 6: "Barack Obama's remarks at the Democratic convention." usatoday.com. July 27, 2004. www.usatoday.com/news/politicselections/nation/president/2004-07-27-obama-speech-text_x.htm

p. 8: Ripley, Amanda. "A Mother's Story." *Time.* April 21, 2008.

pp. 11, 14: Obama, Barack. *Dreams from My Father.* New York: Three Rivers Press, 1995.

p. 12: "Obama's Sister: He's Always Been 'Larger than Life.'" NPR.com. December 27, 2007. www.npr.org/templates/story/story.php?storyId=17640524

p. 15 (top): Boss-Bicak, Shira. "Barack Obama '83: Is He the New Face of The Democratic Party?" Columbia College Today. www.college.columbia.edu/cct_archive/jan05/cover.php

p. 15 (bottom): Karlinsky, Neal, and Dan Morris. "The 'Rat-Ballers': Obama's High School Crew." ABCnews.com. April 26, 2007. www.abcnews.go.com/nightline/Story?id=3082803&page=2

p. 18: Wolfe, Richard. "Barack's Rock." *Newsweek.* February 25, 2008.

p. 19: Schoenberg, Shira. "Law Expert: Obama will preserve Constitution." ConcordMonitor.com. November 4, 2007. www.cmonitor.com/apps/pbcs.dll/article?AID=/20071114/NEWS01/711140429/1217/NEWS98

p. 21: "For Obama, Chicago Days Honed Tactics." WSJ.com. April 21, 2008. http://online.wsj.com/article/SB120873956522230099.html

pp. 24, 28: Associated Press

Index

About the Author

Geoffrey M. Horn has written more than three dozen books for young people and adults, along with hundreds of articles for encyclopedias and other works. He lives in southwestern Virginia, in the foothills of the Blue Ridge Mountains, with his wife, their collie, and six cats. He dedicates this book to Amelia, who asked, and to Marcia, who believed from the beginning.